Cornerstones of Freedom

The Story of
THE PULLMAN STRIKE

By R. Conrad Stein

Illustrated by Len W. Meents

 CHILDRENS PRESS, CHICAGO

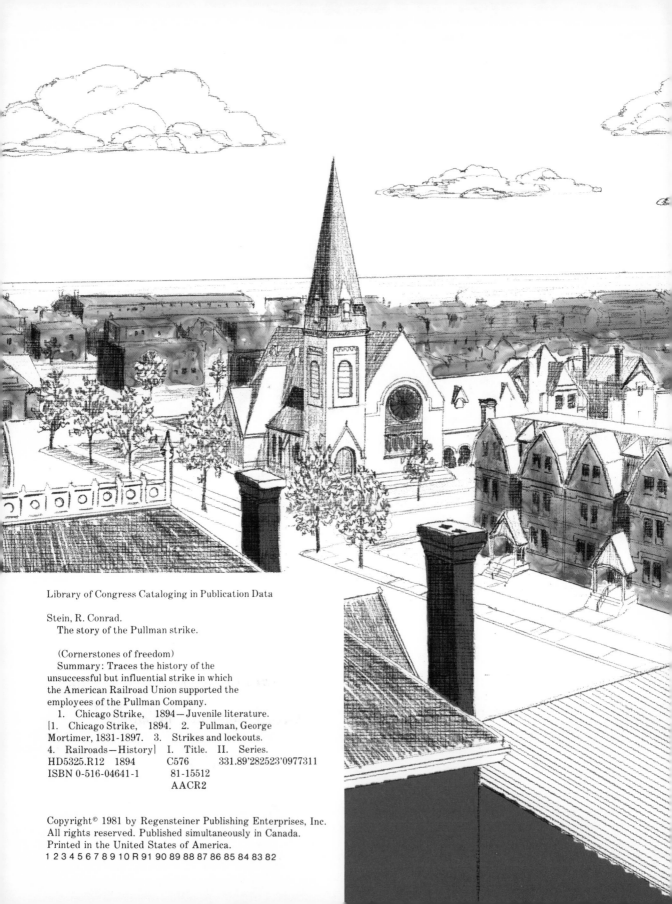

Library of Congress Cataloging in Publication Data

Stein, R. Conrad.
  The story of the Pullman strike.

  (Cornerstones of freedom)
  Summary: Traces the history of the
unsuccessful but influential strike in which
the American Railroad Union supported the
employees of the Pullman Company.
  1. Chicago Strike, 1894—Juvenile literature.
[1. Chicago Strike, 1894. 2. Pullman, George
Mortimer, 1831-1897. 3. Strikes and lockouts.
4. Railroads—History] I. Title. II. Series.
HD5325.R12 1894   C576   331.89'282523'0977311
ISBN 0-516-04641-1   81-15512
              AACR2

In 1893 Chicago held a marvelous World's Fair. Visitors came to Chicago from all over the globe. Most of those visitors rode to the city in splendid Pullman railroad cars.

Near the fairgrounds stood a new city called Pullman, Illinois. Twelve thousand people lived there. The city had rows of red brick houses for the Pullman workers. Tree-lined streets led to a church, a library, a market, and to the factory buildings where Pullman cars were built. Foreigners were especially impressed by the neat little city. One London newspaper reporter called Pullman, Illinois, "the most perfect city in the world."

George M. Pullman had built the new city. He owned the houses and the factory buildings. Pullman had accomplished what most other men only dream about. He had become a millionaire on the strength of a single idea. That idea was to build a comfortable railroad car for passengers. His railroad cars had given Pullman the wealth and power of a king.

But soon after the World's Fair shut its doors, angry Pullman workers walked off their jobs. A huge railroad union supported the Pullman workers. The country exploded into the most bitter strike Americans had ever seen.

The workers rose up against George M. Pullman.

When Pullman was a boy, he probably never dreamed he would some day become rich and powerful. He was born into a poor family with ten brothers and sisters. At fourteen he quit school to go to work.

Pullman was nineteen years old when he took his first overnight ride on a train. That was sometime in the year 1850. The trip was awful. Passengers had to sleep on wooden planks. The railroad provided no blankets. Pullman and the others covered themselves with their overcoats. The car was noisy, dirty, poorly heated, and did not even have a toilet. But the railroad company called this a "sleeping car."

After that ride, Pullman decided that one day he would build a new sleeping car. He hoped to build a car in which passengers could sleep almost as comfortably as if they were in their own bedrooms.

Pullman became a self-taught engineer and a clever businessman. Because of some shrewd business deals, he came to Chicago in 1863 with enough

money to build his new sleeping car. Chicago was then a booming railroad city.

Pullman's first car was called the Pioneer. It was an entirely new kind of sleeping car. During the day, the car had wide, comfortable seats. At night, porters converted the seats into rows of soft beds. The beds were separated by walls. Sleeping in this amazing car was like sleeping in a bedroom on wheels.

It took a year to build the new car. It cost a whopping twenty thousand dollars. The Pioneer was so revolutionary that it would not even run on existing tracks. It was too tall to pass under existing bridges. Its body was so wide that it would smash into existing station platforms. George Pullman said the railroads would simply have to rebuild to accommodate the new car. He was certain that he had built America's future passenger car. And he was right.

Shortly after the Pioneer was completed, President Abraham Lincoln was assassinated. The entire nation wept. But Lincoln's funeral helped George

Pullman. Attached to Lincoln's funeral train was Pullman's car, the Pioneer. Thousands of people saw this new sleeping car for the first time.

In Chicago, Pullman formed the Pullman Palace Car Company. From sleeping cars, the company branched out to build dining cars and private cars for very wealthy people. Success followed success for the Pullman Palace Car Company.

But something happened to George Pullman on his road to success. As he grew richer and more powerful, he hungered for even more money and power.

He forgot that he had once been a workingman.

He began thinking of workingmen as mere tools. They were tools useful only for turning out more Pullman cars.

While Pullman was becoming a millionaire, a man named Eugene Debs was growing up in Indiana. His father was a dreamer who read many books. He often told young Debs that ideas were more important than money. Debs listened to his father closely. Ideas became the most important part of his life. He never learned a love for money.

Debs became a fireman on a train engine. He also joined a labor union. Debs had often seen the families of hardworking men and women go hungry. He hoped labor unions would be able to correct that injustice.

Debs studied the successes and failures of labor unions in the United States. He learned that unions had many enemies. Among their most powerful enemies were the newspapers. At the time, almost every large newspaper in the United States was anti-union. Those papers often lied when reporting the events of a strike. Perhaps one angry worker threw a rock through the window of a company office. The newspapers could easily report that there had been a full-scale riot.

As Debs became a union leader, he cautioned workers about violence. He knew that just one violent act committed during a strike could be exaggerated by the newspapers.

In the 1890s, a depression hit the United States. Companies cut wages and laid off workers. Workers turned to unions for protection. In 1893 Eugene Debs formed the American Railroad Union (ARU). It was the first union to represent all railroad workers from engineers to laborers. Membership spread from coast to coast. In just one year, 150,000 workers joined the ARU.

From his office, George Pullman could look down on the quiet tree-lined streets of Pullman, Illinois. The town seemed peaceful. But in the houses and in the factories the workers were desperate.

The depression had reduced wages in Pullman shops. Yet workers' rents remained the same. Pullman had begun building his town in 1880. The main reason he built it was to make money by renting the houses. The average Pullman worker paid about seventeen dollars a month for his house. The same type of house could be rented in Chicago for about twelve dollars. But the Pullman workers were not allowed to move. It was a company rule that a Pullman worker had to live in a Pullman house.

Pullman even hoped to make money from the town church. A small newspaper, *The Call,* said, "He (Pullman) was not the kind of man who would let you pray for free." But rental on the church was so high that no religous group could afford it. So the church and the parson's house stood empty for many years. Finally, the Methodists raised enough money to pay the rent. A young minister named Reverend William Carwardine moved in. The Reverend Carwardine later defended the rights of the workers against George Pullman.

While the workers worried about putting food on their tables, Pullman showed off his town. He often invited wealthy Chicago families to Pullman. He delighted in showing these people *his* town. He loved to point out *his* people. To George Pullman, the town had become his kingdom and the workers had become his subjects.

In July, 1893, Pullman shops employed 5,500 men and women. By the following May, only 3,300 had jobs. Wages for those still working were slashed 30 percent. Still the rents on Pullman houses remained as high as ever.

Payday at Pullman came once every two weeks. The company deducted rents from the workers' paychecks. The Reverend Carwardine described a company payday in 1893: "After deducting rent, the men invariably had only from one to six dollars or so on which to live for two weeks. One man has a paycheck in his possession of *two cents*. He has never cashed it. . . . He has it framed."

The winter of 1893 was a nightmare for Pullman workers. Children had to be kept home from school. They had no shoes or coats so they could not go out in the snow and ice. Later the children had to be kept in bed all day. Their parents could not afford the coal to heat their Pullman-owned houses.

Meanwhile, the Pullman Palace Car Company was making money. The company had never *sold* sleeping cars to the railroads. Instead, it rented the cars.

During the depression, demand for new cars slowed down. But rental money continued to pour in. In 1893 the company claimed an undivided profit of $2,320,000. So while his workers starved, George Pullman earned more than two million dollars.

Workingmen and women began fainting from hunger at Pullman shops. Groups of workers asked to meet with George Pullman. They wanted to discuss wages and rents. But Pullman refused to see any group of workers. As the Reverend Carwardine later wrote, "It is as difficult for an ordinary man . . . to see Mr. Pullman as for a subject of Russia to see the Czar."

Even some of Pullman's wealthy friends grew disgusted with his stubbornness. Chicago millionaire Mark Hanna said of Pullman, "Anyone who won't meet his own men halfway is a damned fool."

In May, 1894, Pullman employees elected a committee of forty-six workers. The employees threatened to strike if Mr. Pullman refused to meet with the committee. Pullman claimed he had nothing to say. Company foremen however, did talk to the committee. The talks were useless. The foremen could do nothing without the approval of George Pullman. The very next day three members of the

committee were fired. It was rumored that Mr. Pullman had ordered the firings. And that more committee members would soon be fired.

On May 11, 1894, 90 percent of the Pullman work force walked off their jobs. The company laid off the few who remained. The huge doors of the factory buildings were locked. The great Pullman strike had begun.

Three days after the walkout, Eugene Debs visited Pullman, Illinois. Many Pullman workers were members of his union. Debs talked to the workers and met with the Reverend Carwardine. Debs immediately saw the Reverend as a friend. Today it is common for a church leader to fight for the causes of his congregation. Ninety years ago, however, very few ministers would stand side by side with striking workers.

Debs knew the workers alone had no chance to force Pullman to talk. The company was making plenty of money from the rental of its sleeping cars. But what if the sleeping cars stopped running? Debs could order his union to boycott trains with Pullman cars. In a boycott, union members would refuse to work on any train carrying a Pullman car. If Pullman cars were stopped, the railroad companies might refuse to pay rent on them. Then George Pullman would have to talk.

In June the American Railroad Union held a convention in Chicago. Thousands of railroad workers met in a huge hall. Pullman employees spoke to the audience. They told of the high rents and starvation paychecks. A story told by one woman made many workers curse George Pullman. The woman looked thin and tired as she talked. She worked as a seamstress at Pullman. Her father had also been a Pullman worker. He died owing the company sixty dollars in rent. But not even death excused a worker's debt to George Pullman. That sixty-dollar debt was being deducted payday by payday from the paycheck of the seamstress.

Next the convention heard a rousing speech by the Reverend Carwardine. He urged the ARU to boycott Pullman cars. He ended his speech by shouting to the audience, "In the name of God and humanity, act quickly!"

The chairman of the convention asked the union members if they were willing to boycott Pullman cars.

"Aye!" shouted the men.

The Pullman workers had won a great victory. The huge ARU was on their side.

The next day, newspapers all over the country condemned the boycott. The *Chicago Tribune* said the boycott was against the law. "The question of the merits of this or that side of the strike is not pending. The issue is whether Debs shall prevail or the law." From the first day of the boycott, the *Chicago Tribune* called Eugene Debs "Dictator Debs." The newspaper continued calling him by that name throughout the strike.

The boycott worked. It was centered in Chicago. But the ARU had members as far away as California and New York State. Those members refused to work on trains carrying Pullman cars.

Railroad owners were frightened by the boycott.

There had been railroad strikes before. But those strikers had been members of small unions representing only switchmen or firemen. This union was different. It represented all railroad workers. To the railroad owners the ARU was a monster they had to destroy. The owners called on their friends in Washington. Their most powerful Washington friend was a man named Richard Olney.

Richard Olney was the attorney general of the United States. The job of the attorney general is to carry out the law. He is supposed to be fair to those on all sides of a dispute. But Olney was a millionaire who had made his money in the railroad industry. During the strike he became determined to smash Debs and the ARU. And Richard Olney was just as stubborn a man as was George Pullman.

The battle forces of the Pullman strike were clearly drawn. The railroads had money, the newspapers, and the attorney general on their side. The ARU and the Pullman employees had 150,000 workers on their side.

From the beginning Debs tried to prevent violence. He sent dozens of telegrams to union headquarters all over the country. "There will be no violence," Debs pleaded. "One act of violence will

defeat us." "They want us to commit violence." He repeated. "They *want* us to commit violence." By "they" Debs meant the newspapers, the railroad owners, and Richard Olney.

But trouble came. In Hammond, Indiana, an angry crowd halted a train carrying two Pullman cars. The crowd forced the engineer to detach the two cars while frightened passengers watched through their windows. In Cairo, Illinois, fistfights broke out between bosses and workers.

Still, no one had been badly hurt, and there was little damage to railroad property. Somehow the newspapers saw things differently.

Led by the *Chicago Tribune*, the newspapers printed huge headlines:

MOB IS IN CONTROL! LAW IS TRAMPLED ON.

A *Tribune* story began, "Through the lawless acts of Dictator Debs' strikers, the lives of thousands of Chicago citizens were endangered yesterday."

Although there had been no serious trouble, tempers were rising. Violence might break out any moment. George Pullman could have put a stop to this explosive situation. All he had to do was agree to talk to his men. But Mr. Pullman sat in his Chicago mansion. He insisted he had nothing to say to the workers.

In Springfield, Illinois, Governor John Altgeld worried about the situation in Chicago. He had been born in Germany and grew up in a poor, immigrant family. The working people of Illinois had elected him governor. Altgeld hoped to protect the rights of the strikers. But he knew that Debs and the ARU had powerful enemies.

At the time, most of the mail in the country was delivered by train. This gave Attorney General Olney an idea. Olney went to court and asked a judge for an injunction ordering Debs to stop the strike. Olney claimed the strike interfered with mail delivery and free trade. The judge issued the injunction. An injunction is an order from a court. Anyone disobeying an injunction can go to jail.

A later investigation proved that Olney's claim had been false. Mail cars were not being stopped by strikers. Only Pullman cars were stopped.

ARU members were outraged by the injunction. It suddenly made their whole strike illegal. Debs and other officers could go to jail for continuing the strike. An engineer, a fireman, or a switchman could go to jail for refusing to work on a train.

In Chicago, thousands of workers marched to City Hall. They demanded that the injunction be canceled. The demonstration was peaceful. But the *Chicago Herald* said, "There may have been hungry men in Saturday's demonstration, but they were not workingmen. . . . No honest or respectable workingman has time for such anarchistic foolery . . . . Let honest workingmen keep away from these mobs."

The injunction allowed Olney's men in Chicago to hire deputies to keep order during the strike. Everyone knew the deputies would work against the strikers. Loyal workingmen would not take the job. So drifters and vagrants were hired to work as deputies. Those deputies would later cause more trouble than they prevented. The Chicago police chief called them "thugs, thieves, and ex-convicts."

Next Olney wanted President Grover Cleveland to send the army to Chicago. Olney told the president that a mob ruled the city. He pointed out newspaper reports that told of disorder in the streets. President Cleveland believed his attorney general. He ordered federal troops to Chicago.

July 4, 1894, was a strange Independence Day for the people of Chicago. They had read newspaper stories about widespread violence. But no one had seen any rioting mobs. When they woke up on the Fourth of July, however, Chicagoans saw something they could scarcely believe. Soldiers were everywhere. Soldiers marched up and down their streets. Soldiers pitched tents in their parks. Teams of army horses pulled cannons right past their front doors.

In Springfield, Governor Altgeld wrote an angry letter to President Cleveland. Altgeld claimed that

there was no massive disorder in Chicago. He wrote, "The newspaper accounts have in many cases been pure fabrications, and in others wild exaggerations." Altgeld had not asked federal troops to come to the state. He felt as if Illinois had been invaded.

The soldiers were supposed to keep the peace. Their effect was just the opposite. Soon after the army moved in, riots broke out. Mobs attacked railroad yards. Hundreds of people overturned boxcars, looted freight, and set sheds on fire.

A commission later investigated the violence. Witnesses said the rioters were "street gamins" and "hoodlums." One witness told the commission, "I should say those engaged in turning over the cars were largely hangers-on in the saloons and low dives which can be found on both sides of those tracks." The witness added, "I did not see a railroad man engaged in any rioting there."

Debs had told his men to commit no violent act. In spite of their anger, the members of the ARU obeyed. Others, however, did cause trouble. The newspapers were quick to blame the union. Across the country newspaper headlines read:

VIOLENCE ON EVERY HAND!
DEBS' MOB RULES
ANARCHY IS RAMPANT

Perhaps the worst troublemakers during the disorder were the deputies hired by Richard Olney. The deputies were supposed to protect railroad property. But many broke into boxcars to see what they could steal. Most of the deputies carried guns. Some drank whiskey during the disorders. Chicago Police Chief John Brennan charged that "deputies are shooting innocent men and women."

The violence in Chicago reached its peak on the night of July 6, 1894. Near the stockyards a gang of looters found a train loaded with meat. They broke open the doors of the freight cars. From the nearby neighborhood, hungry men and women swarmed over the cars. They fought each other trying to take home some of the meat. Troops fired into the crowd. People fell dead and wounded.

All over Chicago, fires lit the night sky. Troops fought with mobs in a dozen different railroad yards. Shots rang out. Blood spilled.

During the rioting, Eugene Debs pleaded with the people to go home. No one listened. The mobs were not made up of the working people Debs knew. They were young hoodlums caught up in the excitement of a riot. They were Olney's deputies looking for something to steal. They were trigger-happy soldiers who should not have been sent to Chicago in the first place.

In the ruins of a railroad yard Debs looked around him. He saw overturned freight cars and burning buildings. Debs bowed his head. He knew the Pullman strike was over. The Pullman workers, the ARU, and he himself had lost.

After two days, rioting ended. When the smoke cleared, Chicagoans counted their losses. Twelve people were dead, hundreds had been wounded, and property losses were in the hundreds and thousands of dollars.

The workers knew they had lost the strike. Much of Chicago was a shambles, and the newspapers blamed the ARU. Because of the newspapers, public opinion turned against the union. The Pullman workers had not had a paycheck for two months. Their families were hungry.

Slowly workers began drifting back to the Pullman Company asking for their old jobs. The company took back about three-fourths of its old work force. About one thousand workers were considered "troublemakers" and were never rehired. The workers returned to the same low wages and high rents. But now the company made them sign a pledge. The pledge said the worker would *never* join a union while employed at the Pullman Company. The defeat of the strikers was complete.

Eugene Debs went to jail for six months because he had disobeyed the court injunction. Without his leadership, the once-strong ARU began to break apart. After he was released from jail, Debs joined the Socialist Party. He also had further troubles with the law. As a Socialist candidate, Debs ran for President of the United States five separate times. In 1920 he received almost one million votes for the presidency even though he was sitting in a jail cell at the time.

George Pullman died in 1897, three years after the strike. His grave was covered with tons of reinforced concrete. The Pullman family claimed they feared vandals might damage the grave. But writer Ambrose Bierce said, "It is clear the family in their bereavement was making sure he wasn't going to get up and come back."

The Pullman strike was more than just an industrial clash. It was an upheaval that shook the nation.

Certainly the strike was a defeat for American workers. But sometimes defeat later leads to victory. The American people soon discovered how unfairly the Pullman workers were treated. The people were shocked and saddened when they finally learned the facts about the strike. In future labor disputes, the public would insist that their government protect the rights of workers.

The town of Pullman is now a part of Chicago. To his credit, Mr. Pullman built houses that still stand strong today. Many of those houses are now owned by workingmen and women. Some of the present owners are restoring the insides of the old Pullman houses. It is remarkable that workers today can afford to buy and restore the same houses once rented by the struggling workers of the Pullman Company.

Most American workers now enjoy a high standard of living. Perhaps their improved life is a result of the bitter lessons learned during the Pullman strike of 1894.

About the Author

R. *Conrad Stein* was born and grew up in Chicago. He attended the University of Illinois, where he earned a degree in history. He later studied at the University of Guanajuato in Mexico.

History is Mr. Stein's hobby. He is especially interested in the history of the city of Chicago. He was delighted when Childrens Press asked him to write this book about the Pullman strike.

Mr. Stein is married to Deborah Kent, who is also a writer of books for young readers.

About the Artist

Len'Meents studied painting and drawing at Southern Illinois University. After graduation in 1969 he moved to Chicago. Mr. Meents works full time as a painter and illustrator. He and his wife and child currently make their home in LaGrange, Illinois.